FORGOTTEN

GRIEF

A grandmother's struggle to cope
after the loss of her grandson

by Ann Arnold

In loving memory of my gorgeous
grandson George

31st August 2016 – 7th February 2017

St Helena Hospice

St Helena helps local people face incurable illness and bereavement, supporting them and their families, friends and carers.

They also support children and adults who are facing bereavement. They offer the people of North Essex individual care and total support, regardless of their diagnosis or personal circumstances.

Two thirds of their fundraising comes from the public. They rely heavily on the help and generosity of fundraisers, donors and volunteers.

St Helena has been invaluable to me and my family. All profits made from the sale of this book will go to St Helena. They have supported me beyond belief along my difficult journey of 'forgotten grief'

All profits from the sale of this book will go to St Helena Hospice, Colchester, Essex.

Foreword

Personal thoughts about St Helena Hospice as described by Ash (my son in law) who sadly passed away at St Helena aged 31, Victoria (my daughter) and those of myself.

Ash:

It helps knowing my relative is on the bed next to me. That is how it would be at home.

The hospice is awesome.

It's really homely.

The hospice has done wonders to my life.

Victoria:

I was able to stay nights. There was no limit on how many nights or how long I could stay.

You can come and go as you please.

The dog could stay as well.

My own thoughts:

All members of staff are friendly and supportive whether they be clinical, receptionists, admin. They are all amazing.

I can never thank the bereavement support team enough. They have helped me through some very difficult times.

Nothing is ever too much trouble.

St Helena deserves all the recognition that it gets.

Contents

Introduction

'He's gone.' These words spoken by our son-in-law with Victoria (our daughter) at his side spoke of our grandson George who at the age of five months and seven days had that morning passed away in hospital.

The pain felt that morning and every day since is indescribable. The pain is totally different to any other pain and it never goes away.

A grieving grandmother does not only grieve the loss of her grandchild, but she also grieves for and with her daughter or son. Her own child is hurting and needs comforting, supporting and protecting. A grandmother must therefore stay strong (on the outside) while inwardly she is breaking. Silently falling apart.

I have of course experienced death before, both personally and professionally working as a health care professional. Nothing though can ever prepare you for the loss of a grandchild. We are meant to die before our children, and most certainly before our grandchildren.

Maybe this is why there appears to be a lack of understanding of the ongoing pain, anger, frustration and loneliness that a grieving grandmother feels.

Her own child is hurting and she of course wants to be there to comfort and protect them as any parent would. I would do anything feasibly possible to help ease Victoria's pain; I must stay strong for her.

At the time of writing this book we will, in three months, be approaching the anniversary of George's third birthday. This will be another heart-wrenching day, and one that does not get any easier. The pain of losing George is as strong if not stronger than the day our son in law spoke those words that he had passed away. I have not come to terms with his death or indeed dealt with that part of grief 'acceptance.'

My reasons I believe for this are as previously mentioned the definite lack of understanding of a grandmother's grief. I would not wish this journey on anyone and indeed if you have not experienced such a loss how can you possibly know how I am feeling?

I do feel however that more awareness needs to be made. There needs to be more written around this subject and indeed more support groups available. This for me has been a lonely, terrifying experience and I am sure I am not alone. My grief has most certainly been made difficult by further tragedy within our family (which will be discussed briefly) later within the book.

My main reasons for writing this book are to raise awareness of the pain of losing a grandchild, and the ongoing support and help that is needed. I am hoping that through writing my experience and feelings that I may be able to find that acceptance and move through my journey of grief. I am also hoping to bring comfort and understanding to other grandparents that may be grieving and to let you know you are not alone. Lastly my reason for writing this book is to donate any monies from the sale of the book to St Helena Hospice, Colchester as a way of thanking them for their ongoing help and support

Thank you in advance for taking the time to read *Forgotten Grief.*

Welcome Little Man

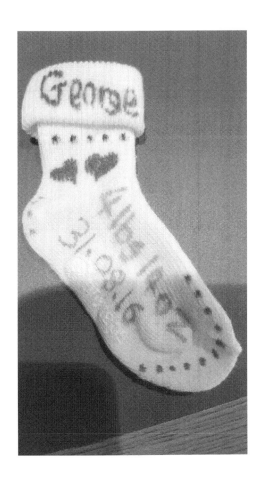

George Kenneth was welcomed into the world on 31st August 2016 with not only the usual excitement of a new birth but also with trepidation. It was known long before his due date that George had many health problems, and his parents (our daughter and son in law) had been told on many occasions that he was not expected to survive. I remember very fondly the evening that George was delivered early by caesarean, and how on being transferred from theatre to intensive care the staff stopped briefly, allowing us to get a look at our grandchild.

He was gorgeous, he was alive, he was fighting. He was small, he had only been with us for a matter of minutes but already I loved him so much. I was a proud grandparent, but we knew the road ahead could be rocky.

We had to take each day a step at a time, and hope beyond hope that our little man could prove the doctors wrong. For a long time that is exactly what he did.

George remained in intensive care but he grew stronger. He melted my heart and I so longed to pick him up and give him a cuddle. This though was not possible. He was still being ventilated and connected to many life-saving machines, but he was alive and he was doing well. That is all any of us could have asked for.

The journey from home to visit George took about an hour each way. His mum and dad lived in the hospital accommodation so they could be close by and live as a little family as much as was possible. They were involved in George's care and I felt immensely proud of how Victoria coped. George suffered the odd relapse but generally he was doing well. One day he would be allowed home, but we all knew that was a long way off. I remember so well the Sunday afternoon that I visited George, and Victoria asked would I like to hold him. Would I? Of course. I held onto him so tightly. He was so precious. I remember the drive home afterwards smiling from ear to ear. I had held my grandson, such a special moment. He was still connected to a heart monitor and oxygen but he was strong enough to be held, he was making progress.

Four days after this on 17th November George had planned surgery. A long and worrying day, once again we asked ourselves will he survive? The operation took virtually all day, but he made it.

Our little fighter continued to go from strength to strength. He was getting too big/too old to be on NICU (Neonatal Intensive Care Unit) so was transferred to the children's ward where his mum and dad could have sleepovers and look after him as if he was at home. Our little man was on the big boys ward.

Reflection 1

Looking back at this time between 31st August-November, I could not have been happier.

Don't get me wrong there were some worrying times, but time and time again George proved the doctors wrong and pulled through infections, blood transfusions and major surgery.

I remember returning home the night after George was born. I could not sleep. I was so excited. I wanted to tell the world. I remember getting up early and going to buy banners and balloons. My phone I think must have been red hot that day informing people of our little arrival. If you are or have ever been a grandparent you will understand my excitement. That instant love is difficult to describe. It is like no other.

Generally we as a society will do anything for our children, for our grandchildren there are no limits.

The days following the birth of George were busy. We looked after Victoria's and Ash's home while they stayed at the hospital as well as our own. I worked three days a week and on days off and some evenings travelled to the hospital to see George. Yes they were busy days but I would not have changed them for the world. I could not wait for those times to go and visit George. To stroke his face, hold his hand and give him a little kiss. That little man was already a huge part of our lives.

I loved him so very very much.

Something is not right

On Sunday 5th February I visited George. My husband was unable to come with me as he was working. George continued to have good and bad days, and it was easy to see on arrival that this was not a good day for him. He was restless and difficult to settle, but what struck me more was my daughter's words.

Victoria was always calm and collected. Nothing fazed her, but today she kept saying something is wrong, he is not right. George was always a happy baby, but today there were no smiles. Indeed it seemed something was not right. The doctors were measuring his oxygen levels and kept popping in and out. All we could do was watch and wait.

Victoria continued to say something is wrong, he is not right. Of course she knew, mother's intuition. Understandably she and Ash were worried, but they needed time together with their little boy. I left that afternoon asking them to keep me informed. I said goodbye to George promising to come and see him again soon.

Throughout that afternoon and evening and indeed throughout the next day Victoria informed us that there was little change.

Reflection 2

Returning home from this visit to see George I remember saying to Graeme (my husband) that George was not himself and that I would not be surprised if he didn't get transferred to ITU (Intensive Care Unit).

George since day one had always needed to be given oxygen to help with his breathing, but today was different. As a nurse and a grandmother I could see things were not right. Victoria instinctively knew this too.

Yes I knew things were not right. I thought he might be transferred to intensive care, but I expected him to pull through as he always had done.

Looking back I believed that he had had a relapse and that he would be stabilised.

The staff at the hospital were amazing. They knew George well.

All the nurses adored him. He had such a cheeky adorable smile. I believed that they would stabilise him again. They would make him better.

The Phone Call

During the early hours of Tuesday 7th February 2017 myself and my husband were woken by the phone ringing. Reaching out to answer it I remember looking at the number that was being displayed. It was not a number that I recognised. I did not recognise the female voice talking to me either, but she knew my name. She explained that she was a nurse from the hospital and that George was poorly. She continued to say that Victoria had asked her to phone us as she wanted us there. I do not remember putting the phone down. All I could hear was those words George is poorly.

George, Victoria and Ash needed us.

The Long Wait

On arrival at the hospital we were taken to a small room where we were given a hot drink and asked to wait. Ash's parents were on their way too, and we were told we would be updated once they had arrived. I am not sure how long we waited for news of our grandson, but it seemed like an eternity.

Outside the room we were aware of the hustle and bustle of staff working, but inside the room all was quiet. Few words were exchanged between us. Nobody knew what to say. Nobody knew what was happening

Suddenly the door to the room opened and in walked Victoria and Ash alone. They were not accompanied by medical staff.

The room remained silent until Ash spoke those words 'He's gone.'

Our little man, our little fighter had gone.

At 07.21 on 7th February 2017
George left us to become the
brightest star in the sky.

RIP Gorgeous Boy

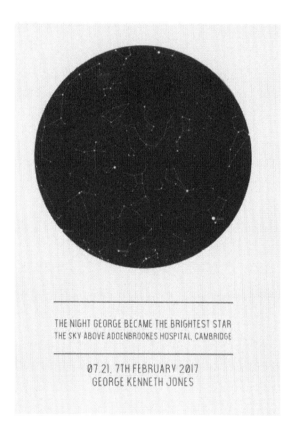

THE NIGHT GEORGE BECAME THE BRIGHTEST STAR
THE SKY ABOVE ADDENBROOKES HOSPITAL, CAMBRIDGE

07.21, 7TH FEBRUARY 2017
GEORGE KENNETH JONES

Reflection 3

How do you look back on such an awful day? It can only be with sadness, tears and heartache.

After being given the sad news we all went with Victoria and Ash to the unit where George was still lying. This was our chance to say goodbye to him. This memory lives with me to this day. I can still see our little man lying there. I don't believe it will ever leave me.

We were allowed to have hand and foot prints of George. A little keepsake which I have in my box at home.

All my memories of George.

We sat with George while Victoria washed and dressed him. I remember a nurse asking me if I would like to help.
I would have loved to, but this was the last thing Victoria could do for

her little boy. I could not deny her that privilege. Unbeknown to me at the time, this was the start of protecting, looking out for my daughter. My own little girl was hurting but carrying on regardless.

In amongst these things I remember phone calls had to be made. Our son and Ash's sister needed to be told the awful news. Other people could be told later, but they needed to be told now.

How did we as a family and individually get through this day? I do not know. I can still see George and the events of the day as clearly as if it was yesterday.

The hardest memory of that day though is Victoria carrying George to the end of the ward, where she had to hand him over to a member of staff for him to go to the mortuary.
I remember her saying 'please make sure he is not alone.' Words that broke me inside.

What an absolutely awful day. I cannot do anything to make things right. I cannot make George better. I cannot bring him back for all of us. I cannot tell my daughter it is ok, it will get better, we can fix this. I CAN'T. As Victoria's mum I am unable to fix things this time. I feel useless.

A grandparent and a parent

Our gorgeous little boy has gone, but I am still a grandmother and always will be. George was and still is a big part of my life, and I will question anyone that thinks otherwise. You do not forget someone just because you can't see them, touch them, hug them, and smell them.

I am of course a parent too and one of the hardest things in all of this is watching your child suffer. I remember the day after George had died and we as a family came home from the hospital. My son cried uncontrollably, just like a baby. He had previously lost grandparents. Indeed death is a natural part of life and it is the expected natural order for grandparents to die first. The loss of a baby is not natural and he clearly did not know how to cope.

Neither did I (I still don't at times), but he is my son. He was hurting. He needed protection, comforting, he needed me. As a mother we tend to be at the forefront of the family unit. We hold things together; we make sure things run smoothly. We try to keep everyone happy, meeting everyone's needs. This does not change when we are facing grief. We have our own pain, we need to find a way to cope ourselves but unfortunately and unintentionally a grandmother's grief is forgotten.

Victoria, Ash, my son and my husband needed me to stay strong. The family unit needed to be maintained. There needed to be routine. This as a parent and a wife is my role. Making sure the family unit doesn't crumble. Everyone is crippled with pain. As the one looked to for guidance, the one who (supposedly) always knows what to do, what to say I must cope.

I must cope especially for my daughter Victoria but also Ash. He must not be forgotten in all this. I am sure he is trying to stay strong for Victoria but he too has lost his son. As parents we must look out for them both, comfort and protect them. They are vulnerable. They may be grown up now but they are and always will be our children.

Victoria is suffering but I feel totally useless. There is nothing I can do to make things better for her, but I am her mum and should know what to do. I need to support my bereaved child while at the same time mourn the loss of my grandson. Many times my own grief is pushed to one side. I must stay strong and positive for Victoria. I worry that if she seems me struggling she will not come to me for help.

No grief is easy but the journey of grief as a grandparent feels particularly hard. I would say the hardest thing I have ever had to deal with.

Family and friends in the early days offered words of comfort, but I don't think they realise the impact this has had on my life. They do not know the intensity of a grandparent's grief. This is not a criticism. They have not walked in my shoes, how can they possibly know. To those that have not walked in my shoes please do not judge me. My grief may seem long. I know I have myself questioned is this normal? Should I be over this by now? Through bereavement support I have learnt my feelings are totally normal and that we all grieve differently. I am not only grieving for my grandson but for my daughter too and this will take time. Some days will be good, while others I know will be bad. I still cry buckets of tears for George. I miss him so much even though I only knew him for a short time. I miss all the things that I know we should be doing with him now.

Talking about George helps and why would we not. As Nancy A Mower (2019) said, *'I resolve to talk about my grandchild as often as I want to. I will not let others turn me off just because they can't deal with their own feelings.'*

So what is grief?

This chapter of the book I can honestly say has been the hardest for me to write. To find the words. What is grief? I don't know. I know that I am grieving, that I suffer daily pain, daily heartache, that I have days when I feel physically sick and struggle with how I am feeling. I am told these are reactions to grief, but ask me to explain it and I can't. Life is no longer straight forward. There are questions to be answered. Why did George die? Why did so much happen to our family? Why can't I have my grandson here to hold? Will I feel like this forever? Again I don't know. Life suddenly feels very complicated.

Wikipedia describes grief as a *'multifaceted response to loss'*, particularly to the loss of someone that has died.

Wikipedia goes on to say that grief also has physical, cognitive, behavioural, social, cultural, spiritual and philosophical dimensions.

Grief has also been described as intense sorrow. The word grief comes from the word *'gravare'* which means *'to make heavy'*. This part makes sense to me and explains my heavy heart.

Grief can also make you feel that you are going crazy. Many times I have asked myself that.

Grief is also loneliness and isolation. My grief has been spoken of at bereavement support but otherwise yes it is locked away during this lonely journey. Society wants us to get back to normal as soon as possible. To go back to work immediately, to get on with our lives and to keep moving. This is exactly what I did.

I needed to support Victoria, to keep the family unit together, to be strong.

I must not cry. If I start crying I don't think I will be able to stop. Slowly I am starting to understand this word grief. It is all the things that I am experiencing, feeling and struggling to deal with. Feelings such as sorrow, misery, sadness, anguish, pain, distress, heartache, torment and agony.

The best explanation of grief for me is that of Maria Shriver (2014): *'It's the opening up to the exquisite pain of absence. It's the moment when you stop trying to move on or change how much it hurts, and just let it out.'*

This I learnt again during my bereavement support at the hospice. It is normal to feel pain after the loss of a loved one. I cannot change what has happened or how Victoria is feeling or how others may perceive me during this difficult journey.

I have to let it out. It is not weak to cry, and cry I did during my bereavement support. Sometimes I cried uncontrollably. So much hurt and pain was being held in. I learnt that I didn't have to be strong while I was there, that I needed to stop and think of me. That I had to let it out.

Yes this word grief is certainly making more sense to me now, but as a society I still don't think it is fully understood.

This I feel is because grief is individual. What one person feels another may not. Kubler-Ross and Kessler (2004) describe five stages of grief, these being denial, anger, bargaining, depression and acceptance. They go onto say though that these stages have been very misunderstood. They are tools to help us frame and identify what we may be feeling. Not everyone though will go through all of these or in this order. I know I certainly haven't.

DENIAL: This stage of grieving is where the world feels meaningless and overwhelming. In a state of shock and denial we feel numb. Sadly while writing this I realise that I still feel like this today. Two years after losing George I still have many times when I feel numb and overwhelmed with emotions, almost feeling like suffocation at times. Do I still feel this because my grief was on hold for so long? Denial helps us to pace our feelings of grief. It is nature's way of letting in only as much as we can handle.

ANGER: I don't think I have experienced anger when thinking of George dying. What has made me angry is the reactions of others regarding my emotions. Nobody's fault. As previously stated, the loss of a grandchild is different to other losses. I would not want anyone to go through this but please don't judge me. Please don't tell me to move on, or that I have to like Christmas and that I have to go out and celebrate Christmas.

My heart is still broken. Underneath anger is pain, my pain. Anger is said to be a strength and it can be an anchor, giving temporary structure to the nothingness of loss.

ACCEPTANCE: This stage is about accepting that our loved one has gone and the reality that they are not coming back. We may not like it, but it is said that eventually we accept it. Where we realise that it was our loved-one's time to die. I understand this stage, but have certainly not reached it. How can it have been George's time to die? He was five months old. It is said that my past is forever changed and that I must re-adjust. This is easier said than done. Acceptance may not happen over days or months. It can sometimes take years. Two years on I still have not reached acceptance. I am still George's nanny, a mum, a wife, a nurse, a colleague and a friend.

I am still the one looked to for answers, taking care of and looking out for everyone.

This still seems to be my role in life. I am at times though still having a rough time. No I don't believe I have as yet found acceptance. I may need to move on. I may need to start living again but I cannot do this until I have given grief its time and this I recognise is what I need to do.

Used with the kind permission of Gary Andrews.
Private Collection. (Unpublished)

Reflection 4

Looking back I questioned so many times is my grief too long, why am I still struggling. Should I be feeling better now? Why don't people seem to understand why I am still hurting so much?

Slowly I seemed to get some answers and make sense of this awful situation. I am double grieving. I am not only grieving for me (for the loss of my grandson). I am grieving for my daughter too. I must look after her. She has to be my priority.

Looking back on the reaction of others around me I can see everyone tried to help me, to make me feel better. I'm not sure though that many people understand this double grief.

Reading experiences of other grandparents that have lost a

grandchild, this sadly seems to be very common.

Looking back, do I think this needs to be spoken of more? More support available? YES I DO, and if possible I would like to be part of improving acknowledgement, support and help around this subject.

Study of grandmothers' grief after the loss of a grandchild

A study carried out by Mental Health and Family Medicine (2018) aimed to describe grandmothers' grief after the loss of a grandchild and to increase understanding of the grief that grandmothers experience and to assist in developing support mechanisms to help them cope.

Throughout the study, data was collected from twenty grandmothers who had lost a grandchild. There were no restrictions on the age or the cause of death of a grandchild. The grandmothers' ages ranged between 40 and 68.

No grandfathers participated in the study.

Data was collected by one open ended question which invited the grandmothers to describe their grief.

On completion of the study and after analysis, results showed that following the death of a grandchild the grief experienced formed a continuous sequence from inconsolable grief to lifelong yearning. The continuous sequence was characterised as crushing emotions, manifestations of grief, loss of energy and a permanent change in one's life.

These feelings are shown more clearly in the chart (Figure 1).

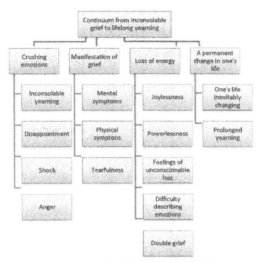

Figure 1. Grandmothers' grief after the loss of a grandchild.

Mental Health and Family Medicine (2018).

Conclusion of report

For grandmothers, the death of a grandchild results in loss of energy and in their lives being permanently changed. In addition to grieving the loss of their grandchild they also grieve the loss experienced by their child. Grandmothers dismiss their own grief and bury it in their hearts.

Grandmothers need understanding and support to cope. More information is needed on the factors that help grandmothers cope with their grief and the kind of support they wish to receive.

More research is also needed concerning the grief of grandfathers and the coping factors specific to them.

My own thoughts on the study

What surprised me when reading the study was that the exact feelings that I have spoken of during my bereavement support were discussed many times throughout the study. This to a certain degree was reassuring. It became apparent that my feelings/emotions were no different to other grieving grandmothers.

Grief was characterised as daily, following grandmothers for the rest of their lives. The pain of losing George is certainly with me every single day. The pain on some days is still unbearable, and I do feel it will stay with me forever. Grandparents have been described as silent grievers, and that their grief is multi-layered.

Again I can strongly relate to this. Sadly eleven months after losing her son, our daughter Victoria also lost her husband Ash at St Helena Hospice. Once again my main concern is of course Victoria. My grief for George still there, but buried deep inside. Fry (1997) wrote that following the death of a grandchild (and in this instance now a son in law), grandparents often provide concrete assistance to their children, to help them cope with everyday life. Victoria is now alone and of course at times needs assistance with certain aspects of daily life. All I want is for Victoria to be happy, but where am I as a grandmother and mother? Our lives have changed permanently. They will never be the same again. Is it wrong for me to discuss my own grief when Victoria has lost so much more? I feel discussing my own grief would be selfish. I need to be there as a parent for Victoria. My grief for George remains buried.

The grief following the loss of a child has been studied extensively from the perspective of the child's parents. This of course is very important. There are however insufficient quantities of studies following the loss of a child from the perspective of the grandparents.

Could this be why I and it appears other grieving grandmothers struggle so much? It almost feels that the subject is taboo. We must not be seen as weak.

I am hurting though and surely keeping things bottled up is not helping. I do not want sympathy that is the last thing I want. What I would like is more awareness, more understanding of the subject and more support groups. I have been helped through my grief by bereavement support through the hospice, and I can honestly say without this I do not know how I would have coped.

I still cry and still have bad days but support helped me to understand this is normal. That it is ok to cry and that grief takes time. I may never get over losing George. I don't think I will. Through bereavement support I have not been judged, made to feel abnormal or stupid. I will be forever grateful for this support knowing that I was listened to and understood when others may have seen my feelings/emotions as irrational.

This kind of support I realise is not for everyone. Grief is different and we all cope in different ways, but if wanted it should be there along with support groups and help lines. Help also needs to be more readily available through GP surgeries. Unfortunately as we sometimes hear within the NHS it can be a postcode lottery. This is wrong. We all experience pain and hurt regardless of where we live.

Moving on

Since losing George and Ash, my outlook on life has changed completely. As a nurse I know how cruel life can be, how things can change in the blink of an eye, but until you experience it first hand you do not totally appreciate the impact that it has. I am still in intense pain, still unsure why life has been so cruel to us. I still want to talk about George. I love that little boy so much, and that will never change.

None of us knows what the future holds. As a family we can only hope that the coming years will be kinder to us. Certain times of the year are very hard. I know the word hate is a strong word, but I truly now hate Christmas. We spent one Christmas with George in Hospital. We will never have Christmas at home with him.

I struggled with Easter this year. George would have been at the age when we could have done an Easter egg hunt together. Friends spoke of their plans with their grandchildren. I could only listen. Instead I decorated Easter eggs and laid them on George's grave. I also wrote a poem for George at Easter and this can be read towards the end of the book.

I have been helped immensely through bereavement support at the hospice and looking to the future I would like to be involved in supporting others. As a nurse I to a certain degree counsel my patients on a daily basis. I am aware of confidentiality and feel I have empathy. If any good can come out of this it is that I may be able to help and support others.

In the future when the hospice feels I am strong enough I would like to do the course to become a bereavement visitor as a volunteer.

In the meantime if anyone at the hospice or elsewhere feels there is a need for a support group for bereaved grandparents I would like to be a part of this. We as grandparents not only need to get the message out there, we need to be able to support each other too.

Reflection 5

Looking back at the time that I have spent writing this book it has been a time of mixed emotions.

It has brought to the forefront some very hard and painful memories, and I openly admit that some of the words have been written with tears rolling down my face.

It has made me realise how much George went through, but I can honestly say that apart from the last day I saw him alive he was a happy little boy. He had the most gorgeous dark eyes and a cheeky smile that not only melted my heart, but also the nurses that cared for him. Thinking of his smile and character makes me smile and to this part writing the book has brought some happy memories.

His mum and dad coped so well, both very strong people. The sad thing is though that Ash is no longer with us, I do know that Ash would be happy for this book to be written and to give something back to St Helena.

On reflection, the last three years have been extremely hard. Not only for me, but as a family. We are all coping (or appear to be coping) in different ways. I am so grateful to the person that encouraged me to contact St Helena for bereavement support. I know help in the future will be there if needed.

Looking at life differently, I want to be able to give comfort to and help others. Is it time for a career change, I have certainly of late been contemplating it. If I can be given the opportunity in grief or bereavement support, who knows?

Strange as it may sound, writing this book has made me realise that I have been lucky. Some people yearn for grandchildren, but never have them. I was lucky enough to have George even if it was for a very short time. I have lots of photos of him (you wouldn't believe how many). I have his hand and footprints. I have some of his teddies but most of all I have some beautiful memories.

George was always drawn to the colour yellow. Summer days are made easier by planting mainly yellow plants/flowers in our garden. We have a special part of our garden which is just for George where there is a child's bench and a sign that hangs on the fence made by myself. This and the memories are what help to get me through. We only had George for a short time, but we had him and for that I will be forever thankful.

When considering is the loss of a grandchild different to other losses? I believe yes it is. It is not openly spoken of. It is double grief. It is hidden grief. Sadly for me and I can only assume for other grandparents too it is *forgotten grief*.

Poems and thoughts for George

On days that have felt hard and extremely painful I have found comfort writing my thoughts down in my **'Angel Journal'**.

I have also written poems for George.

Some of these personal thoughts are shared on the following pages.

Crying isn't weakness

Crying isn't weakness
Admitting grief is strong
This long and windy path of grief
Feels hard and often long.

Support is oh so vital
In whatever shape or form
To let us know we're not alone
And what we're feeling is the norm.

Easter 2019

Decorated Easter eggs
Are scattered all around
Around the house and garden
Just waiting to be found.

Excitement is in the air
I hear your screams of joy
A day of fun and games are planned
For our gorgeous little boy.

The Easter bunny's been at work
He's hidden all the treats
A sprinkled trail of jelly beans
Lie in the springtime heat.

I feel your little hand in mine
I see your warming smile
A day of joy and happiness
If only for a while.

A day of joy and happiness
That is sadly not to be
You'll spend Easter day in heaven
And not down here with me.

No sprinkled trail of jelly beans
No little screams of joy
No planning lots of fun and games
For our gorgeous little boy.

Instead though George I'll do my
best
To stay strong and oh so brave
As I gather painted Easter eggs
And lay them on your grave.

Lots of love little man

Nanny xxx

Extract from my Angel Journal

Grief Never Ends (2014)

Grief never ends, but it changes
It's a passage, not a place to stay
Grief is not a sign of weakness or a
lack of faith
It's the price of love.

18/01/2019

The passage is very long George,
but if grief is the price of love then I
must continue along the passage. I
love you more than you will ever
know.

X X X

God saw you getting tired

I stood at the front of the church and read this well-known funeral poem on the morning of George's funeral. The true author of the poem is unknown. Many said I would not do this, I would not cope. It was hard but I was determined to do it. This was the last thing that I could do for George.

God saw you getting tired
When a cure was not to be
So he wrapped his arms around you
And whispered come to me.

You don't deserve what you went through
So he gave you rest
God's garden must be beautiful
He only takes the best.
And when we saw you sleeping So peaceful and free from pain
We could not wish you back
To suffer that again.
So today we say goodbye George
And you take your final rest

God's garden must be beautiful
He only takes the best.

SLEEP TIGHT BABY BOY

X X X X

And finally

I would like to thank each and every one of you that has purchased this book and taken the time to read it.

For me this is such an important subject. One that I hope you may never have to experience, but if you sadly do I hope that the words within this book may help and offer you some comfort.

I still struggle at some point throughout every day. A certain song, a photo, a certain date, sometimes for no apparent reason.

I will never forget George. He will forever be a big part of my life. I love him so very much.

I hope that through the hospice in time I am given the opportunity to undertake their training to become a bereavement visitor, and that through my own experiences I can listen and support others.

Through purchasing this book you have supported St Helena allowing them to continue supporting people with incurable illness and their families in North Essex.

And just when you thought I had nothing more to say

Before finishing there are some very special people that I need to say a big thank you to

Graeme (my husband)

Thank you for supporting me along this difficult journey. You too have travelled this journey and I know at times have struggled too. You have always been there for me though and encouraged me to do whatever I have needed to do to make dark days better. You have said that by writing this book I have made you proud. Fingers crossed that I can continue to do that by selling copies and helping St Helena as much as they have helped me.

David (my son)

Thank you for your encouragement with writing this book. Many weekends and evenings I have spent tapping away on the computer and you have had to fend for yourself. You have not gone hungry though. You are more than capable of fending for yourself. All I need you to do now is put your hand in your pocket and purchase a copy of the book. You know Ash would want you to!

Friends

Trish, Nicky, Val, Julie B, Julie H, Sue, Rachel, Wendy, Jane, Maggie, Teresa, Shirley and Jen. I'm sure there are others. If your name is not here I apologise but I am truly grateful for all your kind words, the phone calls and the hugs. I know at times I have been distant, but I am truly appreciative of you all.

St Helena Bereavement Admin team

All I can say is thank you as I have said so many times, particularly to Nicky (I'm sure I've been a pain in the bum to you)! You have always helped, forwarded on messages etc and been absolutely great.

Work colleagues

Thank you so much to each and every one of you. I had only been working with you all for five months when George was born. You have supported me throughout and been so understanding. Thank you particularly to Erika and Jackie for our chats which at times I still need but you never complain.

Thank you too for all the help and support with the fundraising for the hospice, which I will continue to do as long as I am able to.

Gill (Bereavement Support)

Thank you so much for your kindness and your flexibility. Nothing has ever been too much trouble for you and you have helped me tremendously. I know I took a while to open up, but once I found that courage you were so easy to talk to. My only regret is that I didn't open up sooner as there was and still is so much to discuss.

Days can still be hard and we know that August will be a very difficult time this year, but I will cross that bridge when I come to it.

You have never once made me feel silly. You encouraged me to write my feelings down, and believed in me when I spoke about writing this book.

Your kindness and support has got me to where I am at the moment and I will never be able to thank you enough.

I truly hope that as time goes on I am given the opportunity to undertake the bereavement support course at St Helena and can help others as you have helped me.

If I am successful in doing this then I can only say if I do half as good a job as you then I believe I will be doing well.

Thank you Gill.

Ash

Thank you Ash for choosing Victoria and making her very happy during your time together. You had your annoying ways, but then don't we all! I could always please you Ash with my chicken pie. Even while staying at the hospital with George you requested a pie next time I visited and of course I obliged. The day that you left us to join George I vowed never to make that pie again and I can honestly say (although requested) I have never made it. That will always be Ash's pie.

And lastly (the hardest 'Thank You' of all, and yes the tears are starting as this is written).

Victoria and Ash

Thank you so much for giving us our gorgeous grandson. We have all experienced so many emotions from elation, worry and sadness. George's life sadly was way too short, but he brought so much happiness and I will treasure those memories forever.

The night George was born, my cuddle with him, the day of his operation, that gorgeous smile, our only Christmas with him. Those memories are locked deep within my heart along with very sad days too. We only had him for a very short time but we had him and I have those memories.

For that, Victoria and Ash, I can only say

THANK YOU.

Rocking an angel to sleep

The heirloom that was never bestowed.

That special part of our garden which is George's garden

References

Aho, A., Inki, M. & Kaunonen, M. *Grandmothers' Grief after the Loss of a Grandchild.* Mental Health and Family Medicine (2018) 13:676-680

Bergen, A. *Grief never ends.* (2014) http://inspirationonline.com/2014/03/grief-never-ends/ Accessed 12th June 2019

Fry P. *Grandparents reaction to the death of a grandchild: An exploratory factor analytic study.* Omega, 1997, 35:119-140

Kubler-Ross, E. and Kessler, D. *On grief and Grieving.* London. Simon and Schuster UK 2014

Mower, N. *The Compassionate Friends.* Volume 36, No 1. 2019

Shriver, M. *On Grief and Grieving* (Foreword) London. Simon and Schuster UK. 2014

Printed in Great Britain
by Amazon